For
Carolyn & Jim
I appreciate you!

[signature]

Oct. 1995

Like A Pelican In The Desert

Leadership Redefined: Beyond Awkwardness

Also by Stephen M. Gower

The Art Of Killing Kudzu
Management By Encouragement

Celebrate The Butterflies
Presenting With Confidence In Public

What Do They See When They See You Coming?
The Power Of Perception Over Reality

The Focus Crisis
Nurturing Focus Within A Culture Of Change

Upsize Selling
Increase Your Sales With The Mix Of Six

Have You Encouraged Someone Today?
366 Ways To Practice Encouragement

Like A Pelican In The Desert

Leadership Redefined: Beyond Awkwardness

Stephen M. Gower

Lectern Publishing
P. O. Box 1065, Toccoa, GA 30577

First edition, published 1994 by LECTERN PUB-
LISHING, P. O. Box 1065, Toccoa, GA 30577.

Library of Congress Catalog Card No.: 94-78477

ISBN: 1-880150-83-2

Dedicated To Dr. Claude Smithmier

For eleven years, you served as my beloved pastor. Thanks for accepting and encouraging me when I was a young pelican in a very big desert.

Acknowledgments

Energy flows in a reciprocal nature. As I speak across the country for leadership institutes and conferences, I find myself not so much giving, but receiving. I am certainly the beneficiary of the energy that flows into me from my audiences of leaders. I would like to here state my appreciation for the legion of persons who care enough about me to follow our initial contacts with a call, a card, a suggestion for improving my presentations and my future books.

I would also like to acknowledge that my pelican in the desert experiences have rarely been travelled alone. To my Heavenly Father, and to my family, to the folk in Toccoa and across the country, to my college students and to my Methodist Men's Club pals, I acknowledge that my most appropriate thoughts are a sum total of your gifts to me!

Mission Statement

The mission of *Like A Pelican In The Desert* is to
provide leaders who are without the experience,
the tutorial touch or the yearning with a unique
guide for redefining leadership and moving beyond the desert that is awkwardness.

Contents

An Introduction

For a good portion of my life, it has been my privilege to encourage the development of leadership skills For the most part, I, my convention audience members and my seminar participants have benefited from the fact that these audience members and seminar participants already possessed a springboard - a base of both expertise and experience. The role of leadership was not a new venture for them.

But today, there is a current of change that anyone familiar with the challenge of leadership must contemplate!

Soon, this current will actually create a new culture of leadership. There are many times when

I feel inclined to confess that this change-current has already surfaced as champion within the minor, if not major, league of leadership.

If the leaders with whom I worked last decade benefited from a solid base - a dual blessing of both expertise and experience, then many of the leaders with whom I now work are "baseless."

If the leaders of the past were blessed with resources called Recollection and Renewal, then many of the leaders of this decade are cursed with calluses named Caution and Confusion.

Recollection and Renewal are parented by elders named Expertise and Experience. Many of this genre contributed to the composite of leadership that has been unfolding over past years.

Caution and Confusion are bred by Anxious and Awkward. Many of this clan helped form the collage of leadership that is now taking shape.

What is the difference between then and now?

Then, many leaders were thrust into a responsibility that was accompanied by an experience - their years of experience. Then, many leaders were placed into positions of power only after they had exemplified a proven potential, an established expertise.

Leadership Redefined: Beyond Awkwardness

Now, through no fault of their own, many leaders are being catapulted into a responsibility that sojourns alone - without the benefit of prior experience. Now, many leaders are being forced to assume the responsibility before the acquisition of a specific leadership expertise.

Why is this happening?

In large part, corporate downsizing is creating this new leadership class. As executives, managers and supervisors are being encouraged, if not sweetly forced, to retire early, a new crop of leaders emerges by necessity - many times without experience or expertise.

Restructuring and reorganization are also trumpeting the call that summons many persons into leadership - before they, the new class of leaders, feel ready!

Naturally, this freshman class of leaders will include many who feel like a "pelican in the desert," out of place - awkward. Admittedly, not everyone will feel this way, but enough identify with awkwardness in leadership to justify, if not mandate, an addressing of the issue!

Like A Pelican In The Desert admits to the significant presence of this awkwardness, addresses the significance of its power over this new legion of leaders and seeks to advance the leaders into a position beyond awkwardness.

The suspicions and skills addressed in *Like A Pelican In The Desert* will also enlighten and encourage the veterans of leadership who are called forth to advise and counsel – to do miracles with this clan of undergraduates.

Finally, anyone who walks the leadership route and at least occasionally trips over awkwardness should benefit.

Like A Pelican In The Desert is divided into three parts: A Definition, A Dissection, A Determination.

Part One, A Definition, seeks to answer the question: "What does awkwardness look like to leaders?" Part Two, A Dissection, seeks to answer the question: "Why is awkwardness so prevalent within leadership today?" Part Three, A Determination, strives to answer the question: "How can leaders move beyond awkwardness?"

Whether you begin our time together as a nervous rookie or as a robust veteran, whether your frustration is entering leadership responsibility without much experience or expertise, or whether your frustration is related to the task of sharing with new leaders your leadership skills, or

Leadership Redefined: Beyond Awkwardness

whether you, in spite of your experience and expertise, still occasionally stumble away from a more satisfying place, I invite you to move beyond awkwardness!

Part One

The Definition

CHAPTER 1

The Loneliness
Of Leadership

For more than a decade, it has been my gift to me!

The therapeutic effect of my helping to broadcast high school football has, in spite of the intensity of the games, been a calming benefit to my hurried mind and spirit. It has proven well worth the rush back from the airport.

Last year, my broadcast partner and I celebrated our one-hundredth broadcast together. Five years prior to our initial broadcast, it was my privilege to broadcast beside this young man's father.

Now, I must make it clear that I have not

been what you would call the "play-by-play" person. For these many years, I have been the "color" commentator for these radio broadcasts.

There is a rather simple reason that explains why I do not do the "play-by-play" - I do not understand the game! Almost anyone listening can tell that, when it comes to the technique of the plays, I have no idea what is going on during the game!

But when it comes to the "color" - the weather, what appears on the scoreboard, when the officials move from short pants to long pants - I know what is happening!

In my element, as "color" commentator, not as "play-by-play" specialist, I am in what my grandparents used to call "hog heaven."

But take me out of that sphere - out of "color" into "play-by-play" - I become lost. That is when I feel very out of place.

My constant cry was: "Please never make me do the 'play-by-play!'"

But, they did! They made me do the "play-by-play" - but I am now convinced that they will never ask me to do it again.

It was late in the season. As had been the case in the past, our team was doing very well. This particular game was a very important play-off contest.

The score was tight. It was fourth quarter. I did know that normally the fourth quarter of a game would be the final quarter. I believe there were about ten minutes left on the scoreboard.

And, that is when he said it! That is when my partner, the "play-by-play" specialist, said it - "I'm sick. I'm going home."

Our conversation went like this:

"You're doing what"?

"I'm leaving. You'll have to do the 'play-by-play'."

"But I do not understand the game"!

"Well, Stephen, that is perfectly clear. It is quite obvious that you do not know what is going on. But I am sick. You'll somehow manage to do fine."

And, amazingly, "fine" is what I thought I had done - until I arrived home.

My wife, still stuck to the chair by the radio, greeted me with: "Do not ask me to go to town with you tomorrow!"

The rest of our dialogue went like this:

"What do you mean"?

"Do you know what you said"?

"No - do you"?

I was about to learn that she did know what

I had said.

I have written it down!!! Stephen, we are a great football team. For years, we have been producing quality players. Several of our players have played professional ball. And one of this year's seniors may soon be a professional football player. And when he scored the game-winning touchdown tonight, when he made perhaps the biggest run of his life, this is what you said. I know, because I have written it down! You said, "There's a man running down the field. Ten men are chasing after him. And I think the one out front is holding something in his hand." Surely, Stephen, you could have done better.

I do not think so. I do not think I could have done better. And, evidently, the station did not think so. I understand that no one ever is to ask me to do "play-by-play" again.

Why did I do so poorly? Why did I feel so inadequate? Why did I feel incongruous, out of place - "like a pelican in the desert"?

I felt out of place because I was out of place. A responsibility was thrust upon me. But, there was no experience, no confidence, no real desire to travel along with the responsibility - I was experiencing something that did not feel good at all!

Awkwardness

What does awkwardness look like?

On that night, awkwardness looked like a "color" commentator trying to do the "play-by-play." It did not look nor feel good! And, it certainly did not sound good!!

That night I had to face awkwardness - I did not do very well!

But day after day, leaders have to face awkwardness. *Like A Pelican In The Desert* is an attempt to help them move beyond awkwardness. But, before we move beyond awkwardness, we must face it. For our purposes, awkwardness has at least three different faces.

The face of awkwardness can look like any of the following:

the responsibility minus the experience,
the tutor minus the touch,
the years minus the yearning.

The Responsibility Minus The Experience

Awkwardness can look like one who is thrust into responsibility without experience. And this is happening all over our country.

Downsizing and the related early retirement that can accompany downsizing can catapult hundreds of thousands of persons into a leadership position that equals responsibility minus experience. They have been given the leadership authority - they have never been given the leadership experience.

In addition to downsizing, and perhaps even related to downsizing, restructuring and reorganization can demand new leaders. The demand can take place before these new leaders feel they are ready.

The Tutor Minus The Touch

Awkwardness can look like one who is asked to teach his or her leadership skills to another person.

This one who has been assigned the role of

tutor has the leadership experience. It is experience that has never included the ability to train or teach others.

The veteran leader feels awkward trying to teach skills he or she has - but skills he or she has never had to teach before. Here the leadership role is expanded to include teaching - teaching to those who may soon be the replacements, the new leaders.

Contrary to popular opinion, there are some people who feel that "doing it" is much more comfortable than "teaching it." Comfort is something that comes to these veteran leaders when their contribution is limited to "doing" not "teaching."

Thrust as leaders into the tutorial role, the "doers" experience the awkwardness of trying to do something - something for which they just do not have the tutorial touch. It has become a case of task experience minus training or teaching experience.

This awkwardness issue is complicated for the veteran leader when he or she is hurriedly instructed to prepare new leaders just as restructuring and reorganization are rushing in!

The Years Minus The Yearning

Not only do those persons who are thrust into leadership responsibility minus experience feel awkward, not only do those veteran leaders with responsibility, experience, and the new tutorial challenge minus the teacher's touch know how awkwardness feels, there is also a legion of folk who have the years of experience but now, for one reason or another, no longer have the yearning to lead.

Something has robbed these veteran leaders of their yearning! It may be the cultural change. It is perhaps the composite of events. It could be a callousness of spirit.

When you take away the yearning, leadership becomes awkward.

The cause of awkwardness could be one of the following: The culture of change, the composite of events, a callousness of spirit.

The Culture Of Change

Anyone who observes polls and markets and graphs, anyone who notices the mood swings of the adolescent, anyone who experiences the distinct, four seasons of Northeast Georgia understands the genre of change.

Change can inspire; it can intimidate. Change can create; it can destroy. Change can lead to assurance; it can lead to awkwardness!

And, change can certainly take away, or enhance, the yearning!

Many leaders, blessed with the presence of years of experience and cursed with the absence of the yearning, are now greeting severe awkwardness for the first time in the culture of change. On this occasion, change appears to have the upper hand.

Sometimes, when new twists are prevalent, they actually wring out the yearning.

The Composite Of Events

Experience can wear two faces. It can be friend or villain; it can be ally or enemy. Experience can actually equal the clarity that is a paradox.

Experience can be a gift - a gift that is a companion to responsibility.

Experience can also be gut-wrenching - a

composite of events that becomes so demanding, so heavy that it leaves veteran leaders feeling as if they have been worn down.

This sheer weight of experience can actually take a toll on the leaders. Here, the massive composite of events debilitates rather than nurtures, detracts rather than enhances, leaves the leader feeling awkward, not assured. It has all been just "too much."

A Spirit Of Callousness

The level of awkwardness can rise in proportion to the presence of a cynical, if not callous, spirit.

Sometimes, leaders feel like "pelicans in the desert" when they know that deep down there is a conflict between what they expect and what they exemplify. They feel awkward inside when they compare their own behavior to their demands. An awareness of a lack of integrity can become internalized as an awkwardness that is externally revealed in harshness and excessive confrontation.

On the other hand, this demeanor of callousness can be created when leaders become perpetually perplexed by the poor performance of those who follow. Whether it is ineffectiveness or ineptness, the attitude and behavior of the follower consistently fall below the expectations of the leader.

At this point, the normally complacent leader reaches the point where he or she can take no more. A cynical and awkward spirit of callousness has been birthed within a formerly compassionate leader. And, the callousness eventually takes away the yearning.

Moving Beyond

You learn a lot on a tramway!

She must have heard it on three different occasions. Nevertheless, immediately prior to the shutting of the doors, indeed as they were already half-closed, she decided to enter the train. She became caught. We helped her. And, she replied: "They should have someone standing there to help you!"

Well, what they did have, and what she flatly ignored thrice, was a system that methodically and redundantly mandated the following: "Caution - These Doors Do Not Rebound Or Spring Back!"

But Leaders Can

Yes, although those train doors would not rebound or spring back, leaders can. Leaders can rebound; leaders can spring back!

Leaders can move beyond the "caughtness" or trap of awkwardness. Leaders can move beyond loneliness.

Once awkwardness is defined, leadership can be redefined in such a way as to allow for the development of the experience, the presence of the tutorial touch and the return of the yearning.

Worded another way, the experience can come; the tutorial touch can appear; the yearning can rebound and spring back.

The pelican does not have to stay in the desert!

CHAPTER 2

The Arena Of Awkwardness

What happens when you put a pelican in the desert? What occurs when the pelican dives to scoop fish and there is no water, much less any fish? What does the pelican do when those webbed feet make contact with desert sand? And that pouch, that unusually shaped pocket designed to hold all the fish – what do you think the pelican does with that thing?

Well, I guess he feels rather awkward! But, I further imagine that the pelican would try to adapt. It is my suspicion that he or she might encounter some difficulty. But I certainly suspect there would be an effort.

The diet might change from crawfish to cactus. The pouch might become a container for water if the webbed feet are able to take the pelican to that very secluded spot.

Enough about the pelican - what does the capacity to adapt have to do with leadership? What does the capacity to adapt offer those who do battle in the arena of awkwardness, feel that awkwardness will inevitably deliver the knock-out punch, and ultimately choose to throw in the towel?

Finding A New Use

If you were to ask me what is the favorite spot in my backyard, I would have several spots to share with you.

But, if you were to ask me where in the backyard is the spot I most frequently visit, I would without hesitation respond that I live a significant portion of my "yard days" around my compost pile.

There is no doubt that my compost pile helps the daffodils and the daylilies, the tulips and the tomatoes, the azaleas and the asparagus.

But - it helps me, too!

It Is Good For Me

Yes, my compost pile is good for me. Every time I see my pile I can be reminded afresh of what I call The Principle Of Adaptability: There Is Another Use.

Another Use For Awkwardness

Now, the point I seek to make here is that there is another use for awkwardness.

Awkwardness can certainly equal the incessant frustration, the departure, the stop!

And awkwardness can actually become not an exit door away from leadership, but a new entrance door into leadership.

This new entrance door takes us beyond Awkwardness toward Effectiveness. In other words, we find another use for awkwardness. It actually becomes a tool that works for us in the area of redirection and growth.

There are many similarities between my compost pile and the redefined leadership that can carry one beyond awkwardness. Remember, this awkwardness can initially take several shapes: the responsibility minus the experience, the tutor minus the touch, the years minus the yearning.

While we are talking about awkwardness and my compost pile, I find myself wishing that you could have seen it a couple of weeks ago.

It contained: weird-looking vines that seemed to wiggle themselves up toward the heavens, my zucchini that had grown four sizes too big, egg shells that had remained intact for four months because I had not crunched them, an eclectic combination of coffee grounds, tomato peelings, grass clippings and some unusual stuff that looked like a blend of daylily leaves and kudzu.

When I think of that compost pile, I not only think of that awkward and eclectic mixture of mostly dying, dead and post-dead, smelly stuff, I also think of something more important.

When I ponder that compost pile, I think of the principle of adaptability and the challenge to find another use - because my compost pile is made of very adaptable and useful stuff.

The oversized zucchini finds another use and eventually helps mulch the oak leaf hydrangea during next year's hot summer. The coffee grounds that helped me start my day all last month will six months from now help me start an asparagus bed.

Leadership Redefined: Beyond Awkwardness

Ultimately, it is not merely a principle of decomposition that I celebrate here; it is the matter of adaptability: the enigma of the start, what looked like the end, and a new start.

Oh yes, the cycle that leads to and beyond my compost pile - my gold reservoir that equals both a mulch and a soil enhancer - is exciting, if not amazing!

The cucumber vines adapt from cucumber manufacturers to delivery boys for next year's blueberries. The zinnias that were so prolific this year will add a zest to next year's crop of cannas. And, the ugly vine that jumped like monkeys all over my daylilies this year will next year become a soil enhancer for a monkey of a different genre - the new crop of monkey grass.

This Is The Exciting Thing

What happened within my compost pile can occur deep within leaders who experience awkwardness.

The collage that is all of your awkwardness and frustration can be thrown into a pile, then channeled from awkwardness into effectiveness. Leadership can actually be redefined in such a way as to encourage leaders to accept and then move beyond awkwardness.

There is a technique that can allow you to find another use for awkwardness.

Here, leaders move toward a state that will serve to enhance the soil that equals growth. Here, leaders will be able to mulch that growth in leadership from a tender state toward confidence - toward a plant, a leader, that stands tall.

My compost pile represented all that equaled a start and the enigma of an ending that was really not an ending. It also equaled a new start. The collage of your awkwardness can equal the totality of your start, the enigma of what you felt to be an ending that was actually not an ending, and your new start.

It all begins with the principle of adaptability and the discovery of a new use. Your awkwardness does not have to remain your enemy. Your awkwardness can actually become your friend. Your awkwardness does not have to impede growth in leadership; your awkwardness can enhance growth in leadership. As you find another use for your awkwardness, as you perceive your awkwardness as blessing, not curse, you can actually position yourself for growth in leadership.

Leadership Redefined: Beyond Awkwardness

The technique of taking your awkwardness and piling it into a compost pile and then finding another use for that awkwardness will benefit from an approach that has at its center a very special guidance system.

Our Guidance System

How does the pelican find its way out of the desert? Or, perhaps more realistically, how does the pelican make his way in the desert? He needs a guidance system.

How does the leader find his or her way out of awkwardness - the responsibility minus the experience, the tutor minus the touch, the years minus the yearning? Or, perhaps more realistically, how does the leader make his way in the awkwardness - and ultimately beyond the awkwardness?

He or she must find a guidance system!

A Major Factor

It was admittedly rather scary. We had been waiting for almost half an hour on the runway when the pilot indicated that the major radar device at the airport was malfunctioning, necessitating twenty-mile intervals between departing flights.

Well, as far as I was concerned, thousand-mile intervals between departing flights would not have made me feel any better about taking off without the major radar device at the airport!

But that is precisely what many of us do in the midst of our awkwardness - we take off without the major radar device working. We flip and flop from disappointment to despair. We encounter the turbulence of disjointedness. We feel as if we resemble the pelican aimlessly meandering in the desert.

Leadership can be redefined. We can define leadership in such a fashion as to help us make a move beyond awkwardness - a move that mandates the presence of a major radar device, a guidance system, that works! This guidance system can become a major factor in our growth.

What Do We Need To Do?

To move beyond the awkwardness, we need to secure a new pair of glasses - very special glasses.

Our guidance system, our technique for

moving beyond awkwardness, our major radar device, equals something that is probably out of your past.

You Had To Give Them Back

That was the only bad thing about it - you had to give them back.

As a child, I found Saturdays to be special, because that was when I could go to Toccoa's Ritz Theater. Now, there were some Saturdays that were not merely special, they were super special!

On these super-duper, special Saturdays, the Ritz would run a three-dimension movie. And, they would give me a very great and powerful pair of glasses! They would call them 3-D glasses.

I imagine that you recall those special days when they would let you wear something that would make it all seem different and more exciting. But, if it was with you, as it was with me, there was a problem.

Earlier, I mentioned that they would give me a pair of 3-Dimension glasses. Well, I guess a better word would be "lend." Yes, I had to give them back. That was the only bad thing about it all. I wanted to take those glasses home!

Well, perhaps you identify with all this. And, if you too wanted to take those glasses home and could not, then I have news for you!

It is as if our major radar device, our technique for moving beyond awkwardness, is a different pair of 3-D glasses. And you *can* take them home! You can take them to work!! You can take them and allow them to help you redefine leadership and move beyond awkwardness!!!

Oh, our pair of 3-D glasses, our major radar device, is not something you wear. Hopefully, it's not only something you read, but something you experience. Please remember, you can take this different sort of glasses home - and to work - and to play - and to leadership!

What Do They Look Like?

Our 3-D glasses look like a combination that emphasizes:
> **Definition,**
> **Dissection,**
> **Determination.**

As we *define* and *dissect* awkwardness, we can find ourselves *determined* to redefine leadership.

CHAPTER 3

Places, Powers, Purposes

The definition of awkwardness has already been explored as: The Responsibility Minus The Experience, The Tutor Minus The Touch, The Years Minus The Yearning.

Now, let us be more specific in the definition of awkwardness. This actually leads to a state where leadership is redefined.

To feel awkward is to feel out of place; to feel awkward is to feel out of power; to feel awkward is to feel out of purpose!

Worded another way, the person minus the place minus the power minus the purpose equals the paralysis!

The Place

The leadership place requires: Vision, Voice, Voracity.

Vision

The leadership place requires vision. Leaders visualize what the compost pile can become. Leaders visualize new uses!

In their mind's eye, leaders see ahead. The one thrust into responsibility minus experience looks ahead in the hope of a new use for this awkward feeling. The one gifted with past experience minus teaching experience looks ahead and visualizes help in the making. The one who possesses the years and is plagued with a yearning absence visualizes how it can feel to once again be in the place of excitement and satisfaction.

To feel awkward is to feel out of place; to feel awkward is to be without vision! Our 3-D glasses will help us visualize! Our major radar device, our guidance system, will help us find our place!

Voice

The leadership place requires voice. Leaders articulate and exemplify their expectations with both authority and authenticity. Leaders possess a place from which to speak. But this leadership podium, minus authority and authenticity, will equal excessive awkwardness; it will actually dilute the voice.

With The Definition, The Dissection and The Determination as our guidance system, we can begin to speak with a voice of authority and authenticity.

The one who now possesses responsibility that is diluted by an absence of experience learns how to transcend from token authority to the authority that is both merited and respected.

With technique in hand, this person begins to feel more at home, more in place, more authentic. He or she speaks with a clearer and more confident voice!

And, remember, authenticity that is programmed into you will come out toward those who work with you as their leader. You will not be able to give what you do not possess. A voice minus authority is a hollow voice.

The one who holds task experience and no teaching or training experience need not linger forever in the land of awkwardness. The 3-D glasses will help him or her learn how to teach or share task experience in a manner that marries authority to an authentic and assured teacher's voice.

The one who possesses the authority that comes with the years, but also possesses the awkwardness that occurs when the yearning has evaporated, has an alternative! The authenticity that has been impaired by a "yearninglessness" can be repaired.

Yes, leaders need voices! The novice, catapulted into leadership responsibility, often prematurely, needs the voice of experience!

The veteran leader gifted with task experience but void of the tutorial touch may be instantly called upon to teach skills to a leadership undergraduate. This person, this veteran leader, will be gifted if he or she can learn to expand leadership skills in such a way that the leadership voice is amplified to include the teacher's voice!

The one who feels as if he or she is losing voice, the one who possesses what I call "leadership laryngitis," the one who has lost the yearning, can learn to speak again.

In fact, if they want to redefine leadership, they must find their voice!

The Voracity

The timidity that accompanies an absence of the experience, the tutorial touch or the yearning, normally does not inspire the tenacity that leadership mandates.

This tenacious approach that springs forth from a voracity, a spirit of committed and determined enthusiasm, is a necessity for those thrust into new or frustrating roles. Without this voracity, leaders become fainthearted! On occasion, they will actually quit. Quite often they will quit before they quit!

The leadership place requires a voracity that vigorously responds to any awkwardness in a manner that leads beyond that awkwardness toward effectiveness and an assuring confidence.

The Power

Let us again briefly visit the issues of authority and authenticity. Since these factors are so dominant as enhancers of the voice that is required in the leadership place, they have already been addressed. But they certainly surface again as we consider leadership power.

Authority Revisited

Here, authority's misuse can equal either *Roughness* or *Reluctance*. In each case, awkwardness is present.

Authority can be taken too far!

The leader can become self-absorbed with his or her power, stuck on this power issue.

The leader's abuse of the authority of power has internal and external impact. This roughness or abuse of the authority that travels with power will ultimately, in most cases, become apparent to the leader, and because the leader is so transparent, it becomes obvious to the team members.

On the other hand, the authority figure who is bashful and reluctant, the leader who feels threatened by his or her own power, or the leader who is excessively dominated by a soft, compassionate and laid-back approach, may begin to feel awkward.

Ultimately, in most cases, particularly those related to the demands of downsizing, restructuring and reorganization, the situation demands the authority that transcends the strategy of the timid!

The Balance Of Power

Power is a matter of balance. Any strength taken too far can become a weakness!

Roughness takes power's authority too far in the fashion of "excessively aggressive."

Reluctance takes power's authority too far in the mode of "consistently hesitant."

If *Roughness* or *Reluctance* are your friends, then you may want to apply the principle of adaptability. You may want to find another use for awkwardness. You may want to discover the balance of power!

Authenticity Revisited

The leadership place demands authenticity. However, even authenticity can be taken too far.

Two examples of Authenticity's misuse are: *Comparative Complainer* and *Redundant Reminderer.*

The *Comparative Complainer* takes his or

her authenticity too far in the following fashion:

> When I compare myself to you, I
> find that I am the genuine one. I am
> the authentic one. Why do you not be-
> have as I do? What is wrong with you?
> Yes, there is a problem - but it has
> nothing to do with me. I am the sincere
> one. Where is your integrity?

The *Comparative Complainer* becomes so preoccupied with his or her own superior sincerity, that he or she becomes little more than a grumbling leader. This grumbling unleashes itself many times in the form of incessant comparison.

Leaders who move beyond awkwardness in the area of their leadership power as it relates to their authenticity cease the comparing.

This "Comparative Complaining" syndrome may explain the loneliness of leadership that many leaders experience. One painful result of comparative complaining is the alienation, and sometimes anger, that followers feel and exhibit toward their leaders.

Redundant Reminderer takes authenticity too far in the following fashion:

> I really care. I really, really do. I
> do not just sign my letters "sincerely" -

I am sincere. I know it may be easier to do it another way, but that would be a violation of my integrity. And, I never, never violate my integrity because I am sincere. I did right, don't you think? I think I did right. I am authentic.

Redundant Reminderer, the habitual horn-tutor, becomes so preoccupied with his or her perceived superior sincerity that the nexus of *Redundant Reminderer's* language is self-centered.

Granted, *Redundant Reminderer's* habitual repetition about his or her sincerity may be an effort of self-reassurance, and even an invitation for reassurance from team members.

But, more often than not, the invitation to reassure backfires and creates an awkwardness in the form of disgust and fatigue on the part of the team members.

Again, it is a matter of balance! Your authenticity is something you do not broadcast. You live your authenticity.

Your negative, if not nasty, complaining, and your rhythmic repetition about your authenticity, can be modified.

Leaders who want to redefine leadership, to apply the principle of adaptability - to cease the complaining and the comparing - do not have to remain lonely.

Again, this caustic and comparative complaining, this incessant repetition, may explain why some leaders feel so lonely.

If you are at least occasionally familiar with the loneliness of leadership, then please remember that authenticity is not something you powerfully, comparatively and repeatedly hold up; authenticity holds you up! Authenticity supports you!

The Purpose

Leaders who redefine leadership will look in two directions. They will look behind; they will look beyond. Unfortunately, many who refuse to redefine leadership consider leadership a discipline that mandates only a glance beyond.

Behind

I become frustrated when it is suggested that the leadership telescope should be exclusively focused toward the future - toward that which is beyond.

The very existence and importance of the compost pile, the presence of understanding as it relates to what we can learn from our awkwardness, and the principle of adaptability, all suggest that our "where we have been" is vitally important.

Our "where we have been," the sum of that which is behind us, actually becomes a springboard, a launching pad, for our growth.

Yes, purpose does not merely look beyond; purpose looks behind as well!

Purpose's Rearview Mirror

Purpose makes heavy use of its rearview mirror. It seems as if purpose is constantly fiddling with, or adjusting, that mirror.

Occasionally purpose will leave the rearview mirror in center position. That location allows for a general view, or overview, of that which is behind.

Generally, this enables leaders to ponder "where they have been." This broad view of the past can be both assuring - "it has been the way it should have been," and curative - "this needs to be modified."

In other instances, purpose will move its rearview mirror toward the right, or tilt it toward the left. It might be repeatedly adjusted back and forth - from right to left, allowing for a more focused view, a glance toward a specific direction.

This allows leaders the capacity to concentrate on a more isolated part of that which can be viewed when one seeks to look behind.

For our purposes, this filtered viewing positions leaders for a glance behind - a glance that has the purpose of viewing what specifically occurred in the past between the leader and his or her awkwardness.

Worded another way, in *Like A Pelican In The Desert*, we want to consider "purpose in leadership" as that which includes a consideration of how you, and perhaps others, have interacted with awkwardness in prior circumstances. This "backward glance" can prepare us for a leadership that has been personally redefined.

How Do You And Awkwardness Get Along With Each Other?

We have three options here. We can relate to awkwardness by responding:
"It seldom happens."
"It often happens."
"It always happens."

Seldom

Some selectively look for awkwardness as they glance in their rearview mirror. They may claim that they were unable to find any significant amount of awkwardness in their past. They might suggest that most every decision and action was a breeze.

I certainly do not fall into that category. I do not know, have never known, and doubt I ever will personally encounter anyone who has never experienced awkwardness. But I do suspect that there are some persons who do feel as if they seldom have a chance to capture their own awkwardness in the rearview mirror. Their perception is that the driving of their life has been trouble-free, smooth-driving, without much awkwardness.

Often

Many of us will admit that when we glance backward toward our past we discover many sensations of awkwardness. Admission here, rather than denial, is rather helpful. When one admits that one encounters awkwardness on a fairly regular basis, rather than rarely, one is positioning oneself for a move beyond awkwardness and a leadership that can be redefined.

Always

Some actually glance into their rearview mirror and never see anything but awkwardness. Their every "rear view" seems awkward.

It is as if the needle has become stuck within the groove that is the record of their past. Needles that are stuck will mandate a redundancy, or a repetition, of the same old thing - the same old awkwardness.

Our Goal

Our goal is not to move beyond awkwardness to the degree that it never happens again.

Leadership Redefined: Beyond Awkwardness

Our glance behind - our purpose of looking back - does not include the unrealistic, "never an awkward moment," leadership style.

We want to move "beyond awkwardness" - not totally away from awkwardness, not distanced forever from awkwardness.

I suspect some awkwardness actually keeps us alive and honest and growing - and perhaps even adds a modicum of humility to our existence!

However, if in looking back toward the relationship between you and your awkwardness, you decide to rank the power of awkwardness over you as a "ten," then our purpose is to help you move the destructive power of awkwardness over you from a "ten" to something that more closely resembles a "five" or a "four" or a "three" on the scale of awkwardness.

I doubt very seriously if any of us can for long relate to our awkwardness and its destructive power in such a way as to notice the level on the awkwardness barometer to even approach a "two" or a "one."

I hope you notice the word "destructive" in our prior paragraphs. I intentionally used that term to imply that awkwardness can have more than one type of power over us.

The destructive power of awkwardness can impede, hurt, distract, frustrate.

However, the constructive power of awkwardness can actually serve as an invitation for growth, an agent for at least a modicum of humility, a common denominator between leader and follower.

Awkwardness is not only out to get the best of you; your awkwardness may be out to help you become your best.

But, you may have to change how you think about awkwardness; you may have to alter how you relate to your awkwardness!

But how can you change, if you do not know your "where you have been"? How can you change, if you do not analyze your prior relationship to your awkwardness?

Yes, leadership purpose includes a backward glance - a look behind - that serves as a barometer for ranking both the need for growth and the rate of growth!

Beyond

As important as the rearview mirror is for safe driving's sake, it will lead you toward an accident if you keep your eyes fixed on this rear-view mirror all the time.

As crucial as the rearview mirror is toward your growth in leadership, it will lead you toward stagnation at best and despair and hopelessness at worst if you keep your eyes totally focused on this rearview mirror.

Purpose also looks beyond!

Here, imagination leads to visualization; visualization leads to a decision and a plan; the plan leads to action and to growth!

It does not have to stay like it is! Leadership can be redefined in such a fashion as to allow one to move beyond the control awkwardness has over him or her toward a situation where that one controls awkwardness.

Look ahead; imagine it getting better. Visualize your attitudinal and behavioral responses when you begin to move significantly beyond the desert!

This imagination is not a cure, but it is a start for leaders who possess dual frustrations: "there is no light behind" and "there is no light beyond!"

If awkwardness is so powerful over you now that you feel out of place, out of power, out of purpose, if this lostness, this incongruity, this "feeling like a pelican in the desert," is getting to you - then get to it!

We've defined awkwardness. Now, let's get to it!

Let's tear it apart; let's dissect it. Let's lay it on the table and diagnose it!

And, let's always remember that it does not have to stay like it is!

Part Two

The Dissection

CHAPTER 4

Awkwardness Is The Desert

Open awkwardness up - you will discover the desert! If your awkwardness approaches a "ten," then you are exceptionally familiar with this desert stuff: *dry, barren, big!*

Dry

When awkwardness is really powerful, it can take excitement out of you!

Since we are talking about dissection here, let me share an unpleasant experience with you. Many years ago, I was teaching a public speaking course on the college level. One particular quarter keeps coming to my mind.

LIKE A PELICAN IN THE DESERT

The college was cramped for space. My speech class would meet in a classroom that also served as a meeting place for biology classes. This particular quarter, the biology classes were busy dissecting.

A smell remained with my class all quarter! And it took its toll - on the class, on me. My lectures were dry; the grades were dry. No one looked forward to the class! It was no fun!

Dissect awkwardness; you may discover a dryness. Perhaps, you do not want to go there at all because the awkwardness, the desert, can be no fun. It can be very uncomfortable.

Dissect the desert of awkwardness and you find dryness. You find something that takes the fun and the life and the leadership out of you!

Some medicines can leave you feeling dry in the mouth. A drought in Atlanta may cause your daylilies and azaleas, and even you, to experience dryness. Spend a day alone in the desert and you'll really discover how it feels to have something pulled out of you!

Analyze your awkwardness, dissect your awkwardness, and you'll find something that is dry. Its dryness is so powerful as to take the leadership energy, excitement and effectiveness out of you.

Barren

This particular chapter is being drafted 33,000 feet high on a Delta Jet from Atlanta to Phoenix.

Earlier today, as I was preparing for several speeches tomorrow in Prescott and Phoenix, Arizona, I found myself thinking about the last time I spoke in Phoenix.

I remember it well for two reasons!

The first reason I recall that trip was that one of my children went with me. He obviously remembers it too. When I told him I was going back to Phoenix and that I would be speaking again in Camelback, he said, "Boy, do I remember that place - I've never seen a spread like their buffet." He remembered the buffet; I recalled our time together!

And there is something else I recalled - the second reason I remember that trip. My son and I went on a tour of the desert. Oh, there were many exceptions, but there was certainly a significant amount of barrenness encountered by us as we toured the desert. It certainly did not look like the Northeast Georgia mountains.

There were many pretty sites, but there

was also that barrenness. The plants with which I am familiar would never sprout in that barrenness. Even my compost pile would not prove big enough a miracle for battling the barrenness!

Not only does awkwardness leave you dry and uncomfortable, awkwardness can take you to a barren land. You do not think as well.

Thoughts that would sprout in the midst of certainty and clarity and confidence do not sprout here - in barren awkwardness. The desert of awkwardness appears to produce no offspring.

Creativity that would grow in the midst of excitement and effectiveness will not even sprout up from the barren turf of excessive awkwardness.

Dissect awkwardness; you discover the void that accompanies barrenness!

Big

And, you feel overwhelmed. Whatever they were dissecting in biology class lingered around and affected me and all of my class.

Something goes wrong; it seems to cause other things to go wrong.

Last week, I was carrying one of the children's car to be serviced and repaired. I had been informed that the clutch was acting up. Well, as I was traversing a hill, it really acted up - it acted out, it ran out, it died!

A clutch problem became a flywheel problem. A flywheel problem became a starter problem. All led to an invitation for the wrecker!

Awkwardness piles up; dryness leads to barrenness; barrenness swells to bigness. You become overwhelmed by the size of the desert of your awkwardness.

Dissect awkwardness and you may find something very big. It's big enough to stifle leaders. It's big enough to suffocate desire. It's big enough to strangle initiative. It's big enough to smother effectiveness!

I imagine when you open up your awkwardness, when you dissect and examine it, you see something that leaves you dry. You discover something that impedes your capacity to function with a barrenness, something that overwhelms you with its bigness.

I have seen all of that too. I have detoured and stumbled. I have retreated. I certainly know what awkwardness can do.

And I believe our Heavenly Father can help us with our awkwardness. But I also believe we can cooperate.

LIKE A PELICAN IN THE DESERT

Our cooperation begins with dissection. Our dissection reveals: dryness, barrenness, bigness. It all equals The Gridlock!

CHAPTER 5

The Desert Is The Gridlock

I t happened once. That was enough!

I was at a training conference. A friend who was attending the conference had brought his youngest child, Jacob.

Jacob and I became big buddies. Jacob was three. We would play together during the breaks.

I only remember with clarity one of the things we did together. We rode an elevator together - and it stopped. It stopped before it was supposed to stop - not on a floor, but between floors.

It just stopped - no more noise - no more movement - no more light - no more power.

Well, Jacob helped me get through that experience, but I sure felt caught, trapped, frozen.

The boundaries that the four elevator walls presented me were confining, limiting and very scary.

The desert can be a little like that, can it not? Oh, the caughtness, the loneliness will appear different: it is not four walls, it is miles and miles of frustration. And, it can equal a paralysis - The Gridlock.

Awkwardness can actually be perpetuated! Leaders who experience perpetual awkwardness, the responsibility minus the experience, the tutor minus the tutorial touch, the years minus the yearning, know how it feels to experience gridlock. It can feel as if leaders are caught in elevators.

The Dissection Progresses

Now, let's dig deeper; let's look further into the caughtness, the frozenness that The Gridlock delivers.

For our purposes, The Gridlock, the perpetuation of awkwardness, equals the following: The Generalization, The Rut, The Inadequacy, The Destination, The Laziness, The Obligation, The Confrontation, The Keeping.

The Generalization

Dissect your awkwardness! You may just discover that awkwardness can look like The Generalization.

The Generalization forgets that awkwardness can wear different faces: The Responsibility Minus The Experience, The Tutor Minus The Tutorial Touch, The Years Minus The Yearning.

The Generalization: it denies that those who work with leaders do not all have the same thrust, history, starting points as their leaders and as each other.

The Generalization: it does not allow for a varying range of degrees as it relates to the effect of awkwardness on personalities.

The Generalization: it forgets that leadership styles do indeed vary because ultimately style becomes an extension of one's personality.

Leaders who redefine leadership move beyond generalization.

The reminder formula here is: The Generalization can equal an awkwardness that exists within a framework that generalizes in assuming that we all have the same starting point, the same resting place, and the same destination.

The Rut

Diagnose the cause of your awkwardness. You may discover that this cause looks like a persistent pattern, a staid situation, the personal choice of comfort over challenge or the imposition of the same (comfort over challenge) on you by your superior.

Look towards the very insides of your awkwardness and you may detect the presence of form. You may even perceive the dominance of form over force.

And it can all leave you as a new leader, or as a veteran leader, with a very empty feeling.

Leaders who redefine leadership move beyond ruts.

The reminder formula here is: The Rut can equal an awkwardness that persists because leaders choose ruts rather than renewal.

The Inadequacy

Inadequacy, perceived or real, can dominate the one thrust into a position of responsibility minus experience. It can even impact the veteran leader, confident at the point of task experience, dubious at the point of his or her tutorial expertise.

Inadequacy, upon further dissection, can look like a past failure or even, I do believe, be disguised as a present fear of success.

I remember my first wasp sting. Dad rushed to his car, secured a cigarette and placed a wad of tobacco on my already oversized, and now mega-oversized and swollen, nose.

I inquired why he was doing that and he responded that it was pulling out the hurt.

Well, inadequacy pulls something out. But, it's not the hurt that inadequacy pulls out; it is the potential. Inadequacy will not only pull effectiveness out of a leader, it can pull away the very effort.

This "pulling-out" is not therapeutic. It can actually torture the leader minus the experience, aggravate the tutor minus the tutorial touch, significantly frustrate and impede the veteran leader blessed with a presence of years but a newly acquired absence of yearning!

Inadequacy can pull out, pull away, any measure of prior, and perhaps not fully-developed, confidence. Awkwardness can pull out both the effectiveness and the effort. Take either or both of these away, the effectiveness and the effort, you may discover inadequacy. Inadequacy distorts or destroys the 3-D glasses.

In an environment of awkwardness, inadequacy wants it all. In a habitat where awkwardness is the frequent visitor, or in an environment where awkwardness totally dominates, inadequacy can demand the eyes and the heart and the mind of the leader.

Leaders who redefine leadership move beyond inadequacy.

The reminder formula here is: The Inadequacy can equal an awkwardness that surfaces when leaders choose to focus on inadequacy (no experience, no tutorial touch, no yearning), rather than initiative.

The Destination

Now at this point, our dissection, the dissection that actually leads to a diagnosis, takes a different route.

Here, awkwardness becomes very confused. The source of confusion equals an association that identifies leadership exclusively with destination.

Leadership becomes much more a place to

go than a person to be. Leadership becomes camouflaged as nothing more than success. The process involved, the people involved, do not seem to matter quite so much as the destination. Hence, the leader actually imposes awkwardness on himself, on others, then back toward himself. In other words, awkwardness presents a boomerang effect that mistakenly and incessantly focuses on the destination. Somewhere, somehow, someone, some leader must service not only the destination, but the journey as well!

Leaders who redefine leadership move beyond an exaggerated emphasis on destination.

The reminder formula here is: The Destination can equal an awkwardness that, upon dissection, lingers when leaders excessively emphasize destination over journey.

The Laziness

Once we return to our dissection table, we discover that awkwardness can actually be fed by laziness.

If the destination represents an excessive aggressiveness, even at the expense of everyone else's journey, if we can actually impose this awkwardness on ourselves by exaggerating an emphasis on destination, then awkwardness must also be something that can be self-inflicted by the leaders' laziness.

When leaders incessantly sit around and wait for the experience, sit around and wait for the tutorial touch, sit around and wait for the yearning to come back, they not only fail to move beyond awkwardness. They actually move further into awkwardness. Laziness becomes the propeller!

It is almost ironic. But I want to tell you about something that just happened!

I am on a plane headed toward the west coast. As a matter of fact, just a moment ago our pilot indicated that we were only one hundred and fifteen miles away from our destination. He mentioned that we would soon be making our final approach. I remember hoping that it would not prove to be too final!

But, a while ago, a barefooted woman came up near the front of the plane. I heard her ask the flight attendant where she might be able to find a bathroom. The attendant pointed to an area about eight feet away from the barefooted woman.

Now, to enter this bathroom, the woman would have to walk across the little kitchen area where the attendants prepared snacks and beverages before she actually would reach the restroom. The attendant cautioned this woman against entering the bathroom barefooted. She further stated that the attendants often dropped glasses in this particular area, and some of that glass probably remained on the floor. As a matter of fact, attendants dropped two glasses and one bowl during this flight.

Well, the barefooted woman just stood there and listened to the attendant. As soon as the attendant finished, the barefooted woman started looking toward the restroom. The moment it became available, she walked - "shoeless and sockless" - across the servicing area and into the restroom.

Now, I do not know what was going on with that woman. I do know that she had much more than ample time to go back to her seat, secure a pair of shoes and return to that spot before the room became vacated.

She did not budge from that spot. What she did do was to give the appearance that she was amazingly lazy.

Granted, awkwardness can indeed gift us, awkwardness that we rate on a scale of three or four can humble, direct, teach and inspire. It can actually help build some sort of commonality between us and our other team members. But an awkwardness will find it very difficult to leave a negative ranking of ten when that awkwardness is landscaped with laziness.

Leaders who redefine leadership move beyond laziness.

The reminder formula here is: The Laziness can equal an awkwardness that will persist or actually swell when fueled by a habitual retreat from effort.

The Obligation

As we continue to dissect awkwardness, we may detect the presence of the chain of a constraint that accompanies the feeling of being bound or tightly tied to an obligation. Plagued by an excessive sense of obligation, the desire that can accompany leadership becomes dwarfed.

Demand Over Delight

Yesterday morning, I was in quite a dilemma. I knew I had four presentations to make and wanted to arrive on the west coast early. Accordingly, I left in a hurry.

In the rush to leave Georgia, I had failed to pack my razor. I had hoped my wife had packed it, but she assumed I had - because I always did - but not this time.

At six-thirty in the morning, I asked the woman at the hotel's front desk if she could find me a razor. Our dialogue went like this:

"The gift shop does not open until eight o'clock."

"Well, could you please help me and see if there is a razor around the front desk area"?

"I doubt it. We don't keep them here."

"Would you mind looking"?

"I'll look, but I'm convinced I will not find anything."

Well, she was right. It was as if she was determined not to help me, and she succeeded. Her job seemed to me to be no more than "demand" to her.

Frustrated, I went to breakfast. After breakfast, as I headed back toward my room, I noticed a different woman at the front desk. So, I tried to find a razor for a second time. Our conversation unfolded like this:

"Ma'am, do you think you might have a razor around here? I have to give some speeches today and my razor is about two thousand miles away from here."

"Let me look," she responded, "I think I should be able to find one. It may take a minute or two, but don't worry."

Well, I worried, but I should not have. She found a razor. I then managed to muster the courage to ask for deodorant - the razor was not all that I left at home. She immediately secured the deodorant.

"Ma'am," I said, "how much do I owe you?"

"Today, for you, Mr. Gower, there is no charge."

And, as I walked away, I heard her gently say, "Have a nice day — I hope your speeches go well."

And, I did - I had a very nice day. I had a very nice day in part because I encountered one for whom work was a "delight," not a "demand."

There is a world of difference between leadership that emerges out of a crucible of "demand" and leadership that unfolds within an environment of "delight." When leadership's awkwardness is dissected, the dissection may reveal the

Leadership Redefined: Beyond Awkwardness

source of the awkwardness to be an attitude that perceives the leadership task to be a demand, not a delight.

What does leadership that is birthed by little more than demand look like?

It looks like Chore. When leadership feels like Chore, one is inclined to go back to the days of childhood and the aggravating chores of milking the cow, emptying the garbage, cutting the grass, and even cleaning the dog pen. It was no fun - but, it was something you had to do. Any grumbling on your part might just make the situation worse.

If you did not do the chores, if you did not respond to your parent's demands, there would be no delight - no swimming, no baseball cards, no 3-D movies. The fun was not in the chores. The fun could only follow the chores.

Leadership loses its place, its power, its purpose, when it is perceived as pain, as demand. Leadership's excitement and potential swivel when leadership is relegated down toward doing something you have to do before you have even a hint of the delight immediately involved or the delight that might wait for you down the road.

Awkwardness can camouflage "delight", circumvent "delight" and call attention to leadership tasks as nothing more than "demand."

If leadership has as its destination a "finishedness," a "finality" that opens the door to delight, if the demand or obligation of leadership only leads to fulfillment *way down the road* and never *now*, then leaders feel awkward.

Granted, most leaders understand the concept of delayed gratification, but delayed gratification taken too far can lead to a sense of daily obligation that paralyzes potential.

The awkwardness of the desert here looks like a draining, an exaggerated emphasis on destination. The meaning and the fun are totally wrapped up in arrival, not in journey.

I want the leadership experience to be fun and meaningful for you now - at least to a degree. Perceived as demand, as a task that equals a chore, perceived totally as obligation, not as opportunity, leadership can feel both awkward and awful. Viewed only as demand or obligation, leadership's potential becomes thwarted, leadership's excitement dwindles.

Remember, any strength taken too far can become a weakness. A sense of obligation or demand taken too far can rob leaders of spontaneity, excitement and effectiveness!

Leaders who redefine leadership move beyond obligation.

The reminder formula here is: The Obligation can equal an awkwardness that breeds itself when leaders choose obligation over opportunity.

The Confrontation

When leaders become very efficient at "catching them doing wrong" and almost inept at "catching them doing right," when leaders incessantly confront team members with specificity and affirm team members with vagueness, they give and receive awkwardness in significant proportions. Here, awkwardness may equal a hollowness for the leader, a horror for those who seek to follow the leader.

When leaders forget why people grow, when leaders mistake building someone up with putting someone down, they may begin to feel awkward, if not guilty! Granted, many leaders appear to carry this confrontational style without any apparent baggage of remorse or guilt; but I suspect deep down they know how awkwardness can resemble hollowness or emptiness.

Those who follow confrontational leaders

will tell horror stories that center around antagonists called Aggravation and even Abuse. The impact of excessively aggressive confrontation upon those following is significant enough to cause them to quit, or even quit before they quit.

Upon dissection, the desire to confront will appear as something that certainly can be helpful: time-saving, loss-saving, even life-saving. Those who have the gumption and the grace to confront us may on occasion prove to be our best friends. I well understand that.

However, as the dissection continues to unfold, it may reveal confrontation pursued so excessively that it begins to look more like torture rather than something which is helpful. Excessive confrontation can actually appear as the culprit that creates awkwardness for both the leader and the team member.

Leaders who redefine leadership move beyond excessive confrontation.

The reminder formula here is: The Confrontation can equal an awkwardness that remains when leaders consistently program and emphasize confrontation over affirmation.

Leadership Redefined: Beyond Awkwardness

The Keeping

The way leaders talk can indicate whether they want to keep or share all the authority and all the attention. When the cause of awkwardness is dissected, one may discover that this total keeping of authority, this emphasis on attention as one that should always be focused on the leader, may actually prove to be the germ that causes the problem of awkwardness for team member and leader.

When leaders repeatedly tout themselves as superior, when they use language like "my staff" - not "my team", or "working for me" - not "working with me", one is invited to wonder who the leader is seeking to build up - himself or herself, or the team member.

Leaders must certainly accept and respond to authority. But when they keep every bit of it, when they refuse to delegate, when they refuse the team members the right to claim some ownership of the ideas, they create awkwardness - for the team member, and ultimately for themselves.

Leaders certainly need and appreciate attention. *One* can initially or inevitably equal a lonely number for those in leadership minus the experience, minus the tutorial touch, and minus the yearning. The journey of the leader mandates a servicing that is internal by necessity. Worded another way, the leader must service his or her own journey - a journey that is often thirsty for what is perceived to be a normal amount of attention and affirmation.

But when leaders demand all the attention, all the credit, they begin to create an environment that ultimately equals an island, leaving them insular, isolated and ineffective.

However, when leaders share some of the spotlight of authority and attention, they begin to build a habitat that can leave them appreciated and affirmed as an effective leader. Incidentally, this same habitat will leave team members serviced at the point of their journey!

The Scab And The Scar

Look for the causes of an awkwardness in leadership, you may find that the infection begins with a cut - the cut of assigned authority and attention. And, because the assignment was never blessed with the ointment of sharing, an ugly and oozey, or transparent, scab formed and remained. The scab of totally-kept authority and attention will turn others off.

Leadership Redefined: Beyond Awkwardness

The scab can actually leave a scar - a scar of ineffectiveness on the leader, a scar of frustration and resentment on the team member. But, the scab can actually heal in such a way that no scar remains.

The curative, the ointment, the redefinition of leadership that takes personalities beyond the awkwardness of the desert, equals the sharing.

Leaders who redefine leadership move beyond the keeping.

The reminder formula here is: The Keeping can equal an awkwardness that is perpetuated when leaders choose the keeping of all the authority and the attention rather than the sharing of both authority and attention.

Table Mesa

I noticed an interesting sign yesterday. A meeting planner had picked me up at the Phoenix Airport and was carrying me to our conference site. As we were driving on the interstate, I noticed a rather intriguing mountain. It was a mountain that really looked more like a table.

I kept focusing on that mountain until a green sign caught my attention. It was a sign that would lead interested travelers from the interstate to this mountain that resembled a table.

What specifically intrigued me was the name on the sign beside the arrow - "Table Mesa."

I asked the driver, "Isn't that redundant? Does not 'mesa' mean table?"

He said, "Yes."

And I said, "So it's really called 'Table Table.'"

He nodded in agreement.

Well, let me be redundant here! "Desert Gridlock" equals "Gridlock, Gridlock"!

Remember, the desert equals The Gridlock. The GRIDLOCK equals: The Generalization, The Rut, The Inadequacy, The Destination, The Laziness, The Obligation, The Confrontation and The Keeping.

Part Three

The Determination

CHAPTER 6

The Pelican Equals The Procedure

We have attempted to define the arena of our awkwardness as one where leaders become familiar with situations that can equal the responsibility minus the experience, the tutor minus the tutorial touch, the years minus the yearning. We have even sought to indicate that the awkwardness can equal some combination of the above experiences of frustration.

We sought to capsule the feelings of awkwardness for these leaders in terms that equaled an incongruity or feeling that resembled that of the pelican in the desert. Specifically, we suggested that leaders who experience awkwardness feel: out of place, out of power, out of purpose.

Then, we left the journey of definition and sat beside our dissection table. We analyzed: why awkwardness can appear, why awkwardness can dominate, how awkwardness looks. We diagnosed the causes of awkwardness and the power of awkwardness over us.

We dissected awkwardness. We saw the desert, The GRIDLOCK, spread out on our dissection table. We saw: The Generalization, The Rut, The Inadequacy, The Destination, The Laziness, The Obligation, The Confrontation and The Keeping.

Now, let's get up from the dissection table. I do not want us to leave it. I want us to stand beside our dissection table. We will not remove anything from this table because we will look often at those items upon our dissection table of awkwardness.

But, remember, we are looking at our dissection table on awkwardness, not as a method to hold to it, but with the desire of moving beyond awkwardness that appears exceptionally destructive.

Leadership Redefined: Beyond Awkwardness

With the definition of awkwardness within the catalogue of our mind, with the dissection table at our side, but not over our head, let us now continue our move - a move beyond awkwardness!

We Need A Map

If we're ever going to leave the desert of awkwardness, the gridlock that equals the trap plus the frustration, we need a map. We need some mechanism, a procedure, a technique. We want to help the pelican come home again!

Accordingly, our method for moving further toward a more complete redefinition of leadership, actually becomes *The PELICAN*.

A Seven-Footed Pelican

I know most pelicans possess two feet. Well, this one wears and benefits from seven feet. Our seven-footed pelican is our procedure for moving beyond The Gridlock. Two feet will not cut the sand; it will take seven.

We will call our seven feet:
>   The Pinpointing
>   The Evaluating
>   The Logging
>   The Imagining
>   The Choosing
>   The Applying
>   The Nurturing

Are you ready to take a trip beyond awkwardness? Well, ponder The PELICAN!

The Pinpointing

Beyond The Vague

eep it ambiguous, and you will keep it awkward! Specificity is smart. The doctor will not treat every malady with the same medicine. The doctor isolates the causes and selects a specific response.

In similar fashion, if you are to move beyond awkwardness, you must target the trouble. Keep it vague - you will never emerge victorious over your awkwardness.

Pinpoint it! You will begin the process that actually moves beyond awkwardness! Pinpoint both The Macro-Awkwardness and The Micro-Awkwardness. Pinpoint the problem!

The Macro-Awkwardness

Does your awkwardness equal that of the one thrust into leadership responsibility minus leadership experience? Does your awkwardness look like that of a veteran leader with task experience minus tutorial experience? Do you feel awkward teaching to others what you know and implement so well? Does your awkwardness look like all those years minus any yearning? Does it resemble decades of experience minus desire?

For our purposes, macro-awkwardness can be pinpointed in three ways: *Minus The Experience, Minus The Tutorial Touch, Minus The Yearning.*

Please pinpoint which macro-awkwardness may be dominating you and trapping you in the desert!

Micro-Awkwardness

Pinpoint your macro-awkwardness, but do not stop there. Chisel macro-awkwardness into micro-awkwardness.

The Chiseling Equals The Breakdown Of The Gridlock

As you chisel macro-awkwardness into micro-awkwardness, as you churn and twist it toward a deeper examination of your frustration, you will be taking a first step toward continuing your move beyond awkwardness.

As you chip away at your macro-awkwardness - *minus the experience, minus the tutorial touch, and minus the yearning,* as you explore your micro-awkwardness, you will notice as many as eight micropoints of awkwardness.

Now, you must pinpoint which micro-awkwardness phases belong to you and your awkwardness.

Eight Micropoints of Awkwardness

Pinpoint:

1 - Does your awkwardness exist within a framework that *generalizes* in assuming we all have the same starting point?

2 - Does your awkwardness persist because you have a tendency to choose *ruts* rather than renewal?

3 - Does your awkwardness stay when you choose to focus on *inadequacy* rather than initiative?

4 - Does your awkwardness linger when you excessively emphasize *destination* over journey?

5 - Does your awkwardness hold on when fueled by *laziness*?

6 - Does your awkwardness breed itself when you choose *obligation* over opportunity?

7 - Does your awkwardness remain when you consistently emphasize *confrontation* over affirmation?

8 - Does your awkwardness perpetuate itself when you choose the *keeping* rather than the sharing?

The first step of the pelican procedure is the pinpointing. Our reminder formula is: The Pinpointing equals a state beyond the vague!

CHAPTER 8

The Evaluating

Beyond The Acceptance

After you pinpoint the source of your macro-awkwardness, your major awkwardness, after you locate the source or sources of your micro-awkwardness, you become positioned for evaluation. You do not blindly accept your awkwardness; you evaluate it! Here, after you identify or define your awkwardness, you evaluate:

Why am I in this state?
What can I do about it?

The Why

You pursue "The Why," not because you're trying to beat yourself down. You ask "The Why" so you can move beyond! You ask "The Why" not to pursue the fruitless, but to pursue the fruitfulness of growth that occurs when you pursue the source of inadequacy or ineffectiveness!

Minus The Experience

You have just been thrust into leadership responsibility; you feel awkward because you have no leadership experience. Now, if you choose to, you can focus yourself into greater discouragement by concentrating on why you are in this predicament so much that you badger yourself: "I dropped out of school too early. I was not aggressive enough. I should have been more political." Now, it might be helpful to look momentarily at those reasons. Please do not stare at them too long!

What I'd like to suggest is that you focus on why you have the responsibility. Do not focus on the negative, keep your eyes fixed on the positive: "I probably would not be here if they did not think I could learn the specifics to accomplish my potential."

Why spend a tremendous amount of time and energy worrying about what might happen if things do not work out simply because you do not have the experience?

Leadership Redefined: Beyond Awkwardness

Perhaps it might be more appropriate to evaluate why you focus on the negative. Please consider focusing on the positive - you may well be in a position now that hundreds of thousands of people wish they were in!

Please allow "your why" at least the option to lead to gratitude rather than to grumbling or grouching.

I know this can be tough. I am merely suggesting out of personal experience the damage we do to ourselves when we focus our questioning in a way that resurrects our faults. Focus your questioning in such a way that it reminds you of our potential, your gifts, the opportunity for growth. Please teach yourself this: the direction in which you aim "your why" can lead to destruction or development. Teach yourself this: the direction in which you aim "your why" can lead you to despair or to determination!

The momentum will shift toward your advantage when "your why" leads to at least partial appreciation, innovation, education and growth rather than total frustration.

Minus The Tutorial Touch

It is possible that your history is based on a massive amount of task experience. However, you may hold the opinion that you do not know how to teach that task experience to others.

Evaluate your frustration and fear here.

Are you afraid of embarrassing yourself? Do you actually think you are so important that they will talk about your demeanor or your mispronounced words or your stumbling when they go home to eat supper? If what you are afraid of happening actually happens, then what? Precisely, what is it that has so much power over you?

Evaluate your fear. You may discover it does not have to have the same power over you. Remember, it starts with "The Why."

Minus The Years

Where has all the excitement gone? Have you lost the yearning? Evaluate the source of the loss.

Is it: fatigue, fear, failure, frustration? Remember, if you want to change the "What," you must look for the "Why."

The What

Our second leg of evaluation leads to "The What." We evaluate what options we have. We evaluate what our next move or moves might be.

A more detailed discussion of "The What" follows. For now, it is essential to state that the evaluation must be two-foci: Why am I in this state? What can I do about it?

The second step of the pelican procedure is the evaluating. Our reminder formula here is: The Evaluating equals a state beyond mere acceptance.

CHAPTER 9

The Logging

Beyond The Doubt

Asking "The What" mandates "The Logging." Log your options so you can move beyond the doubt - "I doubt if there is any way out of this desert - beyond the awkwardness." Log your options so you can proceed beyond the awkwardness - "Well, maybe there is hope. "

Basically, you remind yourself that it does not have to stay like it is - "I do have some options."

Well, put them in writing. I am constantly impressed with the therapeutic benefit of writing one's options down.

Option Evaporation

The list prevents the loss of the idea. The list, or log, equals a decision to move beyond doubt.

It is a gutsy call. Once you call for your log, once you list your options in writing, you position yourself for growth. Your options do not evaporate.

You find yourself in a situation that transcends the incessant doubting about whether or not there are positive options for dealing with awkwardness. You think of it; you write it down.

But do not merely log your positive options, log all of your options. Log what you perceive to be your favorable responses and your unfavorable responses.

The First Step

Label your log!

Remember, for our purposes, we have separated awkwardness into three different types. Certainly, there are other breeds of awkwardness genres that relate to the mismatching of personalities and breeds that relate to conflicts or awkwardness that can result within a mix of very similar personalities.

Leadership Redefined: Beyond Awkwardness

However, since we are specifically concerned with awkwardness that surfaces within an arena of downsizing, restructuring and reorganization, we have isolated the breeds of awkwardness down to three: The Responsibility Minus The Experience, The Tutor Minus The Tutorial Touch, The Years Minus The Yearning.

I do think we will find the information related to these three breeds of awkwardness to be very helpful, even if awkwardness appears on the surface to be entirely related to the mismatching of personality, or to the tension that can result when personalities that are "too similar" are thrust into co-leadership responsibilities, or leader-follower relationships.

With that said, we can label our log with one of the following:

1. The Responsibility Minus The Experience
2. The Tutor Minus The Tutorial Touch
3. The Years Minus The Yearning

To simplify, our possible labels become:

1. *Minus The Experience*
2. *Minus The Tutorial Touch*
3. *Minus The Yearning*

If for some reason you feel that more than one label applies to you, you have an alternative.

For example, you suspect that your awkwardness is a marriage between *Minus The Tutorial Touch and Minus The Yearning.* Here, you can either label your awkwardness as that which you perceive to be the dominant one and forget for the time being the second breed of awkwardness. Or, you can carry the procedure out with one awkwardness, your dominant one, and then immediately carry the procedure out with the other awkwardness.

For our purposes, let's stick to one awkwardness at the time. Remember, you can always return and repeat the process with the less dominant awkwardness at a later date.

The Second Step

You sub-label your log. Your sub-labeling will consist of one or several of the eight elements of GRIDLOCK: The Generalization, The Rut, The Inadequacy, The Destination, The Laziness, The Obligation, The Confrontation, The Keeping. By singling out one, or only a few, of these gridlock issues, you are targeting yourself for tailored growth in the area of your micro-awkwardness.

The Third Step

After you label and sub-label your log, you form two columns: least favorable and most favorable.

Under least favorable, you list those options that you consider to be your least favorable responses. Your first listing is what you consider to be the least favorable of all possible responses; your next listing is that response that you would consider to be your second least favorable response. You follow this process throughout your least favorable listings.

Under most favorable, you list those options that you consider to be your most favorable responses, beginning with the one that you perceive to be the most favorable at that time.

Please remember here that the responses you actually choose may include a combination of different "most favorable" responses, a combination of different "least favorable" responses and a co-mingling that equals both "least and most favorable" responses. Of course, your responses may change from time to time.

Finally, you list your specific micro-awkwardness responses.

A Sample Log

LABEL
Macro-awkwardness - an example: Minus
The Experience

SUB-LABEL
Micro-awkwardness issues - examples:
The Generalization, The Confrontation

POSSIBLE OPTIONS

LEAST FAVORABLE
Quit work. Pout.
Angrily confront my supervisors.
Say and do nothing and let it get worse.
Ask for another assignment.

MOST FAVORABLE
Ask for the help of an outside consultant.
Interview those who have similar predicaments.
Ask for tutorial help from a veteran leader.
Take a day off or take a vacation.
Stick with it and learn.
Focus on the positive.
Talk to my parents. Pray.

SPECIFIC MICRO-AWKWARDNESS RESPONSES

1. I remember we do not all have the same starting point.
2. I remember my tendency to confront with specificity and intensity and my tendency to forget to affirm.
3. I find a mentor or coach and allow him or her to help me.
4. I focus on what I have – not what I do not have.

Remember, the log is a very simple and important step in our attempt to move beyond awkwardness as we redefine leadership.

The third step of the pelican procedure is the logging. Our reminder formula here is: The Logging equals a state beyond the doubt.

CHAPTER 10

The Imagining

Beyond Hopelessness

This chapter is short, but it may not be so sweet.

Here, you imagine the hopelessness or caughtness or utter frustration that some responses will bring to you. Here, you look at your logged list. You compare that sense of hopelessness that you receive when you look at some of your options to a sense of hope you imagine you would feel when you look at your other options. You compare how it would feel if you went in one direction as it relates to how it might feel when you choose to go in another direction.

Swapping Temporary Satisfaction For Long-Term Fulfillment

With log in hand, with imagination at our side, we consider how we will feel later - after we have chosen an option or options. This imagination stage serves as a time delay - a cooling off, or a warming up.

Hopefully, it will keep us from making a mistake, from swapping the temporary satisfaction that may travel with an inappropriate response, an excessively angry confrontation of a superior, for the long-term fulfillment of a meaningful working relationship.

This imagination as it relates to various responses, the least favorable and most favorable, may gift us in such a way as to prevent our firing, our demotion, our guilt-ridden frustration.

Swapping Awkwardness With Something That Lies Beyond

The imagination can not only keep us from making a mistake, this imagination can invite us toward a wise choice. Granted, on many occasions, our imagination may have the propensity for running wild. In such cases, it is wise to secure the second and third and fourth opinion of others. It may prove to be that this "second-opinion check" helps us keep leadership issues in balance.

However, aided by the opinion of others, blessed with reality checks and the gift of time, our imagination may just help lead us out of the desert.

This visualization of how it might feel can inspire and ignite a process that may take us out of the desert, out of our current situation, to a state beyond awkwardness - to a redefined leadership.

The fourth step of the pelican procedure is the imagining. Our reminder formula is: The Imagining equals a state beyond hopelessness.

CHAPTER 11

The Choosing

Beyond Indecision

Choose the direction! After you imagine the various responses, you decide on your direction. You can take a more significant move out of awkwardness toward a leadership that has been redefined - by you!

You are not merely going to sit there in the desert. You are going to move - in a specific direction that is designed to take you out of the desert of awkwardness.

At this point, with log in hand, and with a tested and verified imagination at your side, with the confidence that begins to stir within you as your log marries your imagination - you choose!

It's Tough

This afternoon, my wife and I toured the State Botanical Garden of Georgia. We are just now leaving. My wife is driving; I am writing.

Today, I wear the hat of an overwhelmed writer. The afternoon visit to the garden fed both my creative juices and my conviction that it is sometimes very difficult to choose.

A garden will invariably spawn a creativity within me - and it certainly happened again today. Normally a visit to another garden gifts me with ideas for my garden. But today, as I thought about implementing some of the ideas found at the State Botanical Garden, I became "over-idea-ed."

My wife, as is normally the case, said, "Stephen, just pick one or two ideas, work on them, then you can go to another."

But, boy, that is tough! Which one do you pick?

Pick One Or Two

I wanted to say - "Pick just one." But, I understand from a plethora of personal experiences that it's not always that easy. However, the more you carve your options down, the greater your chance for moving beyond leadership awkwardness. Specificity is the secret. Focusing becomes the formula.

The Choice-Act

Now, this choosing is an active choosing. Here, I mean we choose and we act.

Significant contemplation has already taken place. The procedure thus far has gone through maximum checks and balances. We've pinpointed, evaluated, logged, imagined.

Now, we are ready to choose-act! I am not even sure that it is appropriate to say choose and then act. Accordingly, we coin the phrase "choose-act."

We are ready! The choice and the act are now inextricably linked to each other. The act of choosing and the act of beginning to do are not two separate events - they are one! Hence, we do not merely make a choice; we make a choice-act!

We have already analyzed. An extra-long analysis can lead to an exceptional awkwardness within leaders. It's time to implement the choice-act!

Our choice-act will be sculpted on the following anvil: Accept, Notice, Verify, Initiate, Lead.

Accept

Accept responsibility for your time-tested decision. Trust the procedure. Give it your best effort!

Notice

Notice some fresh air. Hopefully, the clarity of a decision will lessen the burdensome awkwardness!

As this particular book is being written, a great preponderance of my clients are experiencing what I refer to as "The Focus Crisis."

Now, I perceive this crisis to be very understandable. I think most of us know how it is to fall out of focus, particularly in an environment that includes reform, ambiguity about reform, downsizing, restructuring and reorganizing. We know how it feels to be in need of replenishment.

Leadership Redefined: Beyond Awkwardness

In particular, a great many of my health care clients have frustration that is linked to reform. But, I state again that the real venom here is not the reform itself, as much as it is ambiguity about reform.

Even if it remains somewhat awkward, awkwardness is sometimes lessened once you move from ambiguity to clarity.

All of this is mentioned to emphasize this. Notice what is happening within you - after you move from ambiguity to clarity. Notice what is occurring within you after you have made a decision. Notice what is already developing as you pursue the choice-act.

Notice that the power of the focus crisis over you is not as great. *The PELICAN* procedure may already be proving to work for you.

Notice what is happening here. Your excitement may already be whetting your parched appetite.

You have made your decision. You've chosen and accepted your option or options. You have noticed a breath of cool air or even a sip of water in the midst of the desert. The crispness of clarity has replaced the staleness of your awkwardness - and you notice it.

Verify

And, others important to you have probably noticed it as well.

I understand that the more insecure of us seek to hold others responsible for our feelings. I certainly do not want to fuel that effort at either manipulation or confrontation.

I do want to emphasize that it can be very affirming and reassuring when those who have shared in our procedure toward growth, notice, articulate and verify our progress. Their support may actually enhance our own verification.

Initiate

Do it. Do not do it after the choice - but simultaneously with the choice. Drink in your own clarity, swallow their support and do it.

Do: stick with your new responsibility and learn and read and get help and listen.

Do: tackle the tutorial task and discover that your nervous energy can actually work for you by your side, not against you, over your head.

Do: deal with your "yearninglessness." Do: seek counseling, talk to peers, pray, ask for another assignment.

Leadership Redefined: Beyond Awkwardness

Move from the logging stage to the choice-act stage. You have "thought-out" your options long enough. Here, you carry out your options. Here, you exercise your options.

Lead

You take the plunge — and you lead! With the leader's place, the leader's power, the leader's purpose as your companion, you begin to take one "webbed" step at a time. The pelican is on the move!

If "Minus The Experience" is your name, you gain a day's, then a week's, then a month's experience. Each day you do not focus on what you do not know, you focus on your full-fledged responsibility. You focus on your growth potential - and you lead. The momentum shifts to your advantage!

If you're called "Minus The Tutorial Touch," you begin to pay the preparation price - the dues of the teacher. You study more, and you worry less about what they think about your style of presentation. You become vulnerable and wise enough to ask for help - and you lead! The momentum shifts to your advantage.

If your name is "Minus The Yearning," you may take a move that transcends the desire for the job to be all over. You may begin to notice a thirst for it to start anew and afresh. The momentum shifts to your advantage.

You have looked into the face of replenishment as one hungry for experience, thirsty for the tutorial touch, starving for the yearning to come back. Yes, you've looked at replenishment eye to eye; you like what you see - and you lead!

Your choice-act is not skewed by an abnormal dose of hesitation. The hesitation that can equal a dullness does not overwhelm you.

As a matter of fact, as you observe your choice-act, you may detect a glowing luster lying at the top of the anvil! This luster equals: The Accepting, The Noticing, The Verifying, The Initiating, The Leading.

And, yes you may be caught by surprise. But you are leading! You are leading in a new and redefined fashion, you are leading with a new vigor. Surely, there may be more stumbling – but you are leading!

Let me add here that the process may lead to another job, a refusal to teach or even to retirement. Even if any of these options become reality, they hopefully have been clarified and blessed by The Choosing and The Pelican Procedure!

The fifth step of the pelican procedure is the choosing. Our reminder formula is: The Choosing plus The Acting equals a state of correction that leads beyond indecision.

CHAPTER 12

The Applying

Beyond Partial Participation

Y es, you are an active participant in leadership - a leadership that has not only been redefined by circumstances, a leadership that has been redefined by you and your new procedure.

You are now applying what you have learned! And, precisely what you discover, or rediscover, actually positions you for advanced application of the principle of adaptability. You've discovered your own penchant for adjusting.

Apply The Adjustment

I must confess that I have noticed myself hurrying to this chapter. I think it may indeed prove to be a nexus in our time together.

For *Like A Pelican In The Desert* has at its very core the concept that is enveloped with adjustment. Not only do we adjust in such a way that moves us from awkwardness to a state beyond the total dominance of awkwardness over us, we must adjust during the process.

Please do not assume that we merely apply the principle of adaptability once during our move beyond the potency of awkwardness. We keep on learning; we keep on applying the adjustment.

The Adjustments

You may have to apply many adjustments during the process. I would like to note four of the most likely invitations to adjust that may come your way as you seek to work yourself out of the desert! I refer to these in-process adjustments as:

> *Confidently Callous*
> *Forever At The Fair*
> *Afraid To Ask*
> *Excessively Determined*

Confidently Callous

Please, do not let it go to your head. You can let it go to your heart - but not to your head.

You have triumphed over the tough. Circumstances did not merely redefine leadership; you redefined leadership!

You redefined leadership in such a way as to fulfill the responsibility minus the experience. You redefined leadership in such a way as to teach your task experience, even though you did not initially benefit from the tutorial touch. You have redefined leadership in such a fashion as to catch the eyes and hearts of your peers. They want to celebrate with you something very specific - your reunion with your yearning.

They want to celebrate with you; they want desperately to celebrate with you. They want to celebrate your new experience, your new tutorial touch, your new yearning!

But, we make it difficult for people to celebrate with us because we are so busy celebrating ourselves out loud. They are hesitant to affirm us because we are so busy affirming ourselves.

All of this redefining, this march out of the desert, has gone to our head. It equals a confident and caustic callousness that distances us from others.

It may leave you proud; it leaves them cold. It's time to apply the adjustment! Even confidence can be taken too far. So, now you have some experience. Share it. Now, you know what the tutorial touch is all about, rejoice in it - but don't let it go to your head. You have discovered the yearning again. Is it leading towards self-absorption? Or, does it lead toward a gratitude that frees you up for a leadership-heart and a leadership-head that emphasizes shared credit, a giving-back of what one has received, a deep and determined gratitude that breeds a warm spirit.

Forever At The Fair

One of the first presentations I ever gave took place in the late sixties. I even remember what I called it: "You Cannot Stay At The Fair Forever."

I also remember the crucible that gave me the idea — it was the carnival that came to Toccoa twice a year. We would go; I would love that part! We would leave; I would not like that part!!

I wanted to stay at the fair forever. It was

fun; the homework that invited me home through my parents' mandates was no fun.

Appreciate your growth. Respond with gratitude and reciprocity. However, sometimes you may need to move on. You may not find yourself needing or wanting to stay with the new leadership responsibility, the new tutorial touch or the new yearning forever.

As you apply in-process adjustments, you may occasionally sense an invitation to move on— away from the fair.

Please remember that pelicans do not always stay in the same place. Pelicans do not even always remain where there is ocean. I guess you would say that is the very reason I am writing this book.

Even if it's fun, even if it's rewarding, even if you have grown out of awkwardness, beyond the desert, even if it all has for a long period of time now seemed right, there may be a danger in staying forever at the fair. I suspect you'll know when it's time to leave the fair.

Afraid To Ask

It blew my mind. Now, I've heard of busy people, normally men who have difficulty stopping and asking for directions - but this beat all I'd ever seen!

I had spoken for the annual convention for the American Health Care Association in Nashville and was hurriedly trying to make my way to the Nashville VA Medical Center for another presentation.

The person taking me from the hotel to the VA Medical Center seemed to have everything under control - until he said, "Do you know where the place is?"

In shock, I responded, "Excuse me!"

"I am not sure where it is," he replied.

Well, I wonder why he waited ten minutes to frustrate me, why he would not earlier admit we were lost, why he aimlessly drove around, why he refused to ask for directions and why he ever decided to be a professional taxi driver. But that is exactly what he was - a professional taxi driver who was unwilling or afraid to ask for directions.

Of all people, you would think professional cab drivers would have the gumption to ask for directions. But, this was not the case with this dude. He finally did use the radio - but that was to ask the dispatcher to call the VA Medical Center and tell them I would be there shortly!

As you apply your newly-selected options, as you process your procedure, you may notice that an adjustment is necessary in the area of your reluctance to stop and ask for directions. Persons who redefine leadership possess the gumption and the grace to ask for help. They can move beyond the fear that births reluctance and refusal to the focus that includes an invitation for help.

This focusing on the reservoir of another's experience can prove very beneficial - if you ask for help. And, remember, when you exhibit the capacity to receive, you not only give yourself a gift, you also bless your contributing, more experienced, partners with gifts. An invitation to help is normally appreciated.

You are benefited; they are helped. It becomes a mutual gifting - a benefit for you and a benefit for the one from whom you are seeking help. But, it becomes nothing if you do not ask for help.

Excessively Determined

Again, any strength taken too far can become a weakness. If you decide to apply the principle of adaptability, to adjust your way out of the awkwardness of the desert, if you choose a specific option, if you give ample time to the decision and to the procedure, your determination can actually be taken too far. Persistence can be a virtue; stubbornness can be a vice.

Sometimes, we choose and act upon options that prove later to be *inappropriate* options. It does not immediately go very well, but we persist.

On occasion, our persistence will pay off. But, in other cases, our persistence leads to a wheel-spinning, an internal combustion that goes nowhere externally. It brings forth all sorts of havoc on us and our team members.

Here, the adjustment called for may be one that mandates an entirely different approach. The adjustment called for here may lead to a second opinion - to their second opinion. And, as much as I hate to say it, it may lead to an adjustment that dictates, "This is not for me."

The wisdom to admit a mismatch, in spite of

all the efforts of definition, dissection and determination, despite all the checks of internal noticing on your part and external verification on their part, mandates both conviction and courage. Here, adjustment may lead to a significant form of redirection; it may even perhaps demand termination.

But, more likely than not, your adjustment may look more like: Confident Callousness, Forever At The Fair, Afraid To Ask! The Excessively Determined leader may, however, feel it necessary to adjust toward redirection or termination.

Adjust-Apply-Adjust

In the prior chapter, we addressed The Choosing as inextricably linked to The Acting. Here, we must state that our adjustment and application are tied together.

This issue of adjusting is cyclical in nature. The adjustment in our thinking about our awkwardness creates a need for a new procedure. We discover and apply that new procedure. Then, however, we make additional adjustments.

It is almost impossible to separate the application and the adjustment from each other. Attempt to do that, and you will be trapped within theory or philosophy. You may actually find yourself quagmired within the desert, certainly not moving beyond the desert.

The sixth step of the pelican procedure is the applying. Our reminder formula is: The Applying equals a state of application and adjustment that carries leaders beyond partial participation.

CHAPTER 13

The Nurturing

Beyond Satisfaction

The early part of our time together included a reference to my compost pile, to its benefit to my garden and to me.

As helpful as my compost pile is, it reaches its maximum potential only when I regularly turn the pile.

Periodically, with the pitchfork as my tool, I turn and stir the pile - the top becomes the bottom, the bottom becomes the top. The two inner layers switch places with each other. Subsequent turnings will oscillate inside layers with outer layers.

I do not leave my compost pile alone. Neither do I merely add to it. I turn it; I nurture it! It works much better that way.

The final step in our pelican procedure is The Nurturing. Turn all of this stuff over and over in your head. Flip-flop the top with the bottom. Focus on one level and then turn the procedure so another level is positioned to receive the bulk of the heat of your effort. And remember, you can only turn one layer at a time.

As you turn your heap, as you switch from The Pinpointing, to The Evaluating, to The Logging, to The Imagining, to The Choosing, to The Applying, as you try to move beyond the desert, you will want to emphasize this final step, The Nurturing.

You will want to nurture your pile with Appreciation Dust and Sincerity Spray.

Appreciation Dust

Occasionally, I sprinkle my compost pile with lime dust. It does wonders. Nurture your move beyond awkwardness with appreciation dust. Spread some of this dust on those who have contributed to your growth. Do not assume that they know that you appreciate them.

And, by all means, save some appreciation dust for yourself. Nurture your decision, nurture your growth.

Sincerity Spray

My compost pile has also benefited when I lightly spray it with water. A light-to-the-touch moisture, not a sogginess, is the goal.

Spray your journey with a sincerity that equals attention to detail, hard work, as well as a modicum of play and relaxation.

A One-Two Punch

Sincerity, coupled with appreciation, may equal a one-two punch that can knock out the macro-awkwardness. Take it seriously, seriously enough to keep it moist, but not so seriously as to make it soggy. Do not allow this to become another example of a strength (sincerity) taken so far that it leads to dullness and a return visit to the desert (additional awkwardness).

Nurture your compost pile. Nurture your move toward a redefined leadership and beyond awkwardness. Use both appreciation dust and sincerity spray.

The nurturing will equal a balance - a balance between an appreciation expressed both internally and externally and a seriousness that is tempered by play and relaxation.

Nurture your team member; nurture yourself! You will even want to nurture your decision to redefine awkwardness and to move beyond the desert with both appreciation dust and sincerity spray.

All appreciation sent their way and none dusted toward you will make for an awkward you. All seriousness and no fun will make for an awkward you.

When you nurture your team member, yourself and your new pelican procedure, nurture it with a balanced appreciation dust and a balanced sincerity spray!

The seventh step of the pelican procedure is the nurturing. Our reminder formula is: The Nurturing equals a state where newness is nurtured beyond prior satisfaction levels.

CHAPTER 14

The
Personalization

As we wrap up our time together, let me tell you about an experience that actually happened more than twenty years ago. It was an experience that continues to occasionally plague me even today.

A friend and I had traveled about one hundred miles to visit a plot of land that was very special. My great-grandmother had owned it for about half a century. Upon her death, it began passing down from generation to generation.

This particular land was blessed with tremendous trees. Upon arriving at the land on that day, my friend and I noticed that one of the very large trees was beginning to die. We knew it would bless our chimneys with superb firewood if we did not let it rot, so we retrieved a chainsaw from the back of the pickup.

As we tried to work our way to the base of the tree, we noticed an abundance of vines that had wrapped themselves around the tree and were wriggling up toward the tree's top. There was no way we wanted to risk an encounter and an entanglement between saw and vine, so for quite a while we pulled the vine down from the tree and out of the ground.

And that was it - now all we had to do was cut, section, split, load and unload the wood. That would be it until fall.

However, that day impacted me for a full month thereafter. Daily, after all of the firewood had been cut, sectioned, split, loaded and unloaded, I still found myself thinking about that tree - and those vines that went up it.

For one month, I battled the worst case of poison ivy I have ever encountered. It seemed that this ivy of poison particularly chose to play havoc with my wrists. I want you to know that to this very day, when I just walk close to poison ivy, the areas that had been disturbed and discolored on my wrists two decades ago will once again become infected by the ivy.

I do not even have to touch it. It made such an impression, impact and injury on my system twenty years ago that, in one way or another, it would be with me forever!

Accordingly, I am very aware that experiences impact us both initially and consistently. The effect of the experiences can be both negative and positive - in many instances, there is actually a co-mingling between the negative and the positive.

The Desert

Once you leave the desert, you have not really left it. If the desert impacted you in certain areas, even another experience that brings you close to, not into, the desert may affect you.

Your pelican in the desert experience can impact you initially and consistently. But, it need not continue to have the same power over you as was the case in your past.

Surely, "experiencelessness" may surface again. "Tutorial touchlessness" may raise its head once more. "Yearninglessness" may once again touch the previously infected spots where the wrists of your leadership had been affected.

But, the power of "experiencelessness, tutoriallessness, yearninglessness" may not be as significant as it once was. And remember, for the poison of your awkwardness to linger around to a degree may not be totally negative.

Your "where you have been" can remind you of your capacity to move beyond awkwardness. It may remind you of your potential to redefine leadership. Do not be surprised if down the road you cannot use again your capacity to move beyond awkwardness. Your "Where You Have Been," your time in the desert, may even lead to a more humble you – a leader redefined by humility.

Do not be surprised if down the road you cannot use again your ability to redefine leadership.

Your memory as it relates to the poison ivy of awkwardness that you previously experienced may serve you well. The redefinition of leadership is something that *you* can constantly nurture!

You

If I could actually talk to you right now, I would use every fiber within my voice to emphasize the pronoun "you" with intensity and inflection. With my voice, I would underline, italicize and articulate in boldness one particular word - "you!"

I have learned how to redefine the power of poison ivy over me. I try to avoid it. This has proven to be almost impossible for one who loves to play in the dirt and the trees and, unfortunately, the poison ivy once again.

I have learned to bless my wrists with long sleeves and gloves. I have tried to carry my ointment of maximum strength Cortisone and my prescription of those highly inexpensive and very effective Cortisone tablets with me.

Accordingly, poison ivy no longer has as much power over me. But, for that to occur, I had to "particularize," personalize, my procedure: the awareness and the distancing, the long sleeves and the gloves, the Cortisone ointment and tablets. Basically, I had to find my way out of poison ivy's dominance over me.

And that is the point I want to leave with you. Ultimately, you must find your way out of the desert.

Just as I had to find my way out of poison ivy's dominance over me, just as I had to find my way through "the play-by-play" side of broadcasting when all I could really do was "the color," so you must personalize the procedure of The PELICAN in such a manner that it helps you find your way.

Now, before we close, I must share this. Please allow me the privilege of being personal, but not offensive. It is my personal experience that the One Who created us and loves us supremely, "Our Heavenly Father," is always available to help us find our way and His way.

Time To Say Good-Bye

I imagine you can notice here again that I am more gifted at saying "hello" than "good-bye." I experience awkwardness when challenge meets closure - but it's football season, and I do have to get ready for another round of "color commentating."

But, as we part, may I wish you the best as you seek to find *your* way - *your* way out of the desert. I hope The PELICAN procedure will encourage you to redefine leadership and move beyond awkwardness.

May you find experience! May you find the tutorial touch! May you find the yearning once again!

Worded another way, and perhaps a better

way, may it all - the experience, the tutorial touch and the yearning - find you! Hopefully, it will begin to find you once you discover this reminder formula: *The Pelican plus The Personalization equals The Progress.*

Do not just discover The PELICAN. Live it! And, take care my pelican friend!

Adaptability

Please look into my face.
Can you tell that I feel out of place?

For you see "Pelican" is my name.
And, somehow I don't feel the same.

Cast into a very strange place,
To feel more normal again, that's my race.

The Desert has become my home,
Here I am not comfortable when I roam.

If somehow I am to grow,
Then, this much I do know.

I must make a friend of this uncertainty.
A much better use must become my remedy.

This awkwardness need not be my enemy,
It can help me be my best me.

For when the Pelican in the Desert I see,
I can discover once again my adaptability.

Stephen M. Gower
Fall of 1994

Notes

Helpful reading as it relates to the awkwardness that I categorized as Minus The Experience can be found in Stephen R. Covey, *The Seven Habits of Effective People.* New York: Simon & Schuster, 1989 and in Stephen M. Gower, *What Do They See When They See You Coming?* Toccoa: Lectern Publishing, 1993 and in Zig Ziglar, *Over The Top.* Nashville: Thomas Nelson Publishers, 1994.

Helpful reading as it relates to the awkwardness that I categorized as Minus The Tutorial Touch can be found in Stephen M. Gower, *Celebrate The Butterflies.* Toccoa: Lectern Publishing, 1993 and in David A. Peoples, *Presentations Plus.* New York: John Wiley & Sons, 1988.

Helpful reading as it relates to the awkwardness that I categorized as Minus The Yearning can be found in Stephen M. Gower, *The Art Of Killing Kudzu Management By Encouragement.* Toccoa: Lectern Publishing, 1991 and in Scott Peck, *The Road Less Travelled.* New York: Simon & Schuster, 1972 and in Pat Riley, *The Winner Within.* New York: Berkley Books, 1993.

Additional beneficial material can be found in the Recommended Reading List that follows.

Recommended Reading

Bramson, Robert M., Ph.D. <u>Coping With Difficult People</u>. New York: Anchor Press/Doubleday, 1981.

Corbin, Caroline. <u>Strategies 2000</u>. Austin: Eakin Press, 1986.

Covey, Stephen R. <u>The Seven Habits of Effective People.</u> New York: Simon & Schuster, 1989.

Decker, Bert. <u>You've Got To Be Believed To Be Heard</u>. New York: St. Martin's Press, 1992.

Drucker, Peter F. <u>The New Realities</u>. New York: Harper and Row, 1989.

Gower, Stephen M. <u>The Art Of Killing Kudzu - Management By Encouragement</u>. Toccoa: Lectern Publishing, 1991.

Gower, Stephen M. <u>Celebrate The Butterflies - Presenting With Confidence In Public</u>. Toccoa: Lectern Publishing, 1993.

Recommended Reading (cont.)

Gower, Stephen M. <u>What Do They See When They See You Coming? The Power Of Perception Over Reality</u>. Toccoa: Lectern Publishing, 1993.

Hanson, Peter G. <u>The Joy Of Stress</u>. Kansas City: Andrews and McMeel, 1988.

Hersey, Paul Dr. <u>The Situational Leader</u>. New York: Warner Communications, 1984.

Huseman, Richard C., and Hatfield, John D. <u>Managing The Equity Factor...or "After All I've Done For You.."</u>. Boston: Houghton Mifflin, 1989.

Johnson, Spencer. <u>The Precious Present</u>. New York: Doubleday and Company, 1984.

Kami, Michael J. <u>Trigger Points</u>. New York: McGraw-Hill, 1988.

LeBoeuf, Michael. <u>How To Win Customers And Keep Them For Life</u>. New York: G.P. Putnam's Sons, 1987.

Recommended Reading (cont.)

McCormack, Mark H. <u>What They Don't Teach You At Harvard Business School</u>. New York: Bantam Books, 1984.

Naisbitt, John, and Aberdeen, Patricia. <u>Megatrends 2000</u>. New York: William Morrow and Company, 1990.

Nanus, Burt. <u>The Leader's Edge</u>. Chicago: Contemporary Books, 1989.

Peck, Scott. <u>The Road Less Travelled</u>. New York: Simon & Schuster, 1972.

Peoples, David. <u>Presentations Plus</u>. New York: John Wiley and Sons, 1988.

Redfield, James. <u>The Celestine Prophecy</u>. New York: Warner Books, Inc., 1993.

Riles, Pat. <u>The Winner Within</u>. New York: Berkley Books, 1993.

Recommended Reading (cont.)

Von Oech, Roger. <u>A Kick In The Seat Of The Pants</u>. New York: Harper and Row Publishers, 1986.

Von Oech, Roger, Ph. D. <u>A Whack On The Side Of The Head</u>. New York: Warner Books, 1983.

Walton, David. <u>Are You Communicating?</u> New York: McGraw-Hill Publishing Company, 1989.

Ziglar, Zig. <u>Over The Top</u>. Nashville: Thomas Nelson Publishers, 1994.

About The Author

Stephen M. Gower is considered one of the country's most powerful speakers. Mr. Gower is nationally and internationally recognized as a specialist in management by encouragement and in the development of communication skills for leadership! His power-packed keynote speeches and seminars have impacted thousands of people across the United States and overseas.

Mr. Gower holds a bachelor's degree from Mercer University and a master's degree from Emory University. He is a member of the National Speakers Association and has taught public speaking on the college level for more than a decade. As founding president of the Gower Group, Inc., and as author, consultant and keynote speaker, Stephen Gower has created a unique approach to human resource development.

Stephen M. Gower's first book, *The Art of Killing Kudzu – Management By Encouragement,* has helped establish him as a national leader in his field. *Celebrate The Butterflies – Presenting With Confidence In Public*, Mr. Gower's second book, reveals a fresh solution on redirecting your nervous energy to work for you as you speak in public. *What Do They See When They See You Coming? – The Power Of Perception Over Reality,* Mr. Gower's third book, addresses perception as it impacts leadership.

Other works by Mr. Gower include: *Upsize Selling – Increase Your Sales With The Mix Of Six, The Focus-Crisis – Nurturing Focus Within A Culture Of Change,* and *Have You Encouraged Someone Today? – 366 Ways To Practice Encouragement.*

Mr. Gower possesses a rare blend of substance, humor and intensity that will excite and energize any audience. Throughout the country, many national and state associations and Fortune 500 companies have invited him to speak. It is not unusual for the same association, corporation, or community to invite him back repeatedly!

The Gower Group, Inc.
P. O. Box 714
Toccoa, Georgia 30577
1-800-242-7404